Accademia di architettura, Mendrisio
Sergison Bates architects, London and Zurich

Contents

This book is a companion to the exhibition I was invited to participate in by Yvonne Farrell and Shelley McNamara, The Practice of Teaching at the 16th International Architecture Exhibition – La Biennale di Venezia. At their encouragement, it explores the relationship between the teaching in the studio I have directed since 2008 at the Accademia di architettura in Mendrisio, Switzerland, and my work as an architect in practice.

I value the collaborative nature of architecture both as an architect and as a teacher. While it is relatively young, the Accademia di architettura has become a significant school of architecture in the global context, thanks to the contribution of a number of remarkable teachers and architects who share a common belief in the culture of building as a primary concern, and a commitment to a humanist tradition.

I have now been teaching for over twenty-five years, in the course of which I have worked with more than a thousand students in various schools of architecture throughout the world. In my work as a teacher I rely on the support of my assistants, whose generous help allows me to do what I would be unable to accomplish on my own. But it is the work of the students that I value most. They generate projects and find solutions to the issues and briefs we set. Their energy and commitment to the discipline of architecture never ceases to inspire me, and it is their work that offers the most tangible account of the ambition of my teaching studio. What is documented in this book is but a fraction of the production of a semester.

When we established our practice in the mid 1990s, Stephen Bates and I believed that it was our complementary abilities that we should draw upon as a basis for working, a reciprocal form of support. For some years we had been collaborating and exchanging ideas with a group of friends – architects, writers and artists – that rather organically came together in London at the time, and the discussions we found ourselves immersed in were instrumental in the development of our own critical position. Twenty-two years later, our own practice counts three partners and thirty collaborators in our studios in London and Zurich. This has greatly enriched the work we produce, to the extent that the authorship of projects is much richer, more complex and ultimately multilayered.

There are a number of other collaborators who continue to play an important role in our work. First among them are Ian Cartlidge and his graphic design studio, Cartlidge Levene. We have been working together for as many years as we have been in practice: sometimes Ian has been our client, sometimes we have been his, and at other times we have collaborated on joint projects. What Ian brings to a project is always surprising, and the design of this publication is a testament to his talent and to his ability to work creatively with others to achieve results no one could aspire to on their own.

Much the same can be said about the photographs by Bertie Miller contained in this book. They are stills from the film by Watermill, London, that will be on show at the Biennale Architettura 2018. The film records my work as a practitioner and teacher of architecture over a six-month period. What comes across clearly is that much of that work is part of the fabric of everyday life and is enriched by encounters, conversations and shared efforts. Through the eyes of the filmmakers the free space where architectural ideas are explored and developed is revealed as fertile ground for dialogue and collaborative endeavour.

The recording of a conversation I had with Irina Davidovici in Zurich in December 2017 is the soundtrack to the film, and an edited transcript of our conversation is included here. For many years I have been provoked and inspired by the questions Irina asks about architecture. In many ways, she is my most demanding critic.

The last component of this book is a collection of texts I have written over the last six months, part of a threefold form of practice that involves building, teaching and writing. While my writing is not intended to be scholarly, it helps me makes sense of what I am attempting to do as an architect, and I hope it may provide some insight to those who take the trouble to read it.

Jonathan Sergison
Zurich, 25 February 2018

Irina Davidovici

The theme of the 16th International Architecture Exhibition – La Biennale di Venezia is Freespace, and I've been thinking of teaching as a free space for the exchanges of information. Teaching is an act that goes both ways and I'm curious to know what you learn from teaching, why you teach…

Jonathan Sergison

I've come to realise over time that teaching has benefits for my own different forms of practice, that is, building, teaching and writing. I've been teaching now for more than twenty-five years and I've been in practice for only twenty-one. That says something about my commitment to teaching, as I started just a few years after I finished my formal education at the Architectural Association. What I have come to realise is that a wonderful exchange occurs through teaching, which creates space for a form of speculation that finds no place in professional practice.

Part of the reason why I teach is that teaching affords me the time and space to have a discussion with a collection of often motivated, bright, energetic and open-minded young people. Exposure to their own investigations has made my own position ever so much sharper year after year. When I first started teaching, I felt instinctively drawn to it as an activity, and in time I have come to realise that it offers the possibility of reciprocity.

I first found myself teaching at what was the North-West London Polytechnic when Micha Bandini had just been made head of school. She said she remembered me as a student of Rodrigo Perez de Arce at the Architectural Assocation School of Architecture, and that I seemed like someone who would be drawn to teaching. She offered me the possibility of learning how to teach as an assistant in her studio. I've come to realise that this was the most wonderful opportunity.

Unlike the hierarchical model of teaching that is generally applied in continental Europe, with a teaching assistant above the students and a professor above the assistant, in the UK young people often find themselves teaching without the benefit of learning from an experienced teacher. They will remember their own formal education, but they won't have the chance of learning teaching techniques. Micha kept her promise, and she did teach me how to teach. There are teaching techniques that I learnt from her which I often find myself falling back on…

Now, many years later, I am teaching at the Accademia di architettura in Mendrisio. I'm one of the design professors and, typically, I have some twenty-four students in my studio. I have relative freedom in terms of the programme I set my students; as long as it conforms to the timetable of the semester, I'm at liberty to set my own teaching agenda. What that allows me to do is to focus on topics I am interested in, which have a connection to practice, but can be explored with a degree of freedom that only exists in a teaching environment.

ID So, you started talking about the relation between practice and teaching. Could you tell me more about how you organise your practice, or rather how teaching informs your practice in more concrete ways?

JS Not an easy question to answer briefly. As a teacher, I believe that the tasks I set students should be useful in their future in practice. And I certainly find myself at odds with a version of teaching, which is quite prevalent in London schools and, to some extent, in North American schools, where the kind of speculation that is encouraged is quite far removed from what is useful.

In my experience, it is so far removed that the transition between the university or school of architecture and professional practice risks undoing what they have learnt. At the same time I don't believe that the agenda that I set in my teaching practice should be wholly preoccupied with the useful aspects of practice. Of course, there is room for a form of speculation which is unburdened by financial contraints, by a real client standing in front of you and by all the other real-life constraints architects experience.

When I started teaching in Mendrisio I though it would make sense to draw upon London as a place for the students to investigate. In part, this seemed logical because London is the European city I know the best, and I would be able to share with the students a knowledge I would not expect them to have of such a vast and urbanistically complex city. Over a number of years we looked at a much wider range of European cities, and one of the bases of my teaching has been an investigation of the architecture of the European city, the urban condition of the European city. As we know, some 70 percent of all of building stock in European cities is housing, and therefore housing has often been the building programme we have focused on in the studio.

ID You mention housing, and indeed residential projects are very much part of your teaching agenda. Now, as a programme, this is an interesting condition to explore. It is both intimate and generic, with a certain number of traits that are replicated across various locations. How do you deal with the overlap between the public and private sphere, between the general and the specific in your teaching?

JS We need to remind ourselves that it was only at the end of the nineteenth century that seriously minded architects turned to popular housing as an area of investigation, despite the fact that it is the prevalent urban typology which shapes the character of a city. It is also very complex. It is important for students to explore the territories and thresholds between the public realm and the privacy of a home, although it is a difficult and sometimes frustrating task. Working on these topics with students, the plan is present but I am much more interested in the way they explore images of housing and place it in an urban situations – in other words, in the representational character of housing.

ID This takes us to the question of how buildings express themselves onto the city. In your teaching you address questions of urbanity and decorum almost in a methodological way, semester after semester. Of course there are variations from place to place, but there is also a more general condition. Loos talked about his own houses, as different from housing: for him the house is a shared space *par excellence*, in the sense that the interior belongs to the private life of the owner, while the exterior belongs to the city. So it is one of these territories of negotiation between private and public. In your students' work there are very extensive explorations of representation in projects. I mean, the representational character of buildings, not the representation of buildings as drawings on paper. Can we talk about that?

JS Your question brings to mind the role of the window in mediating between two opposed but complementary spaces: the interior as a place of privacy and domesticity and the city beyond. It screens the interior, but also opens out onto the surrounding space; it is both a point from which the outside world is observed, and can be in itself an object of observation, part of the spectacle of a facade.

We have often explored this in my teaching studio in the exercises students are set at the beginning of a semester. One exercise requires students to make a carefully measured drawing of an existing building in the city we are working in, and the purpose of this is to achieve an understanding of the building tradition of that place. This helps counter students' tendency to making proposals that are born out of their own intuition rather than rooted in the culture of the place in which we are working. It is a very, very carefully determined approach: the students are given a building and have no choice on the subject. They are asked to stand in front of a building and observe for a length of time what it is that they are really seeing.

As a next step, they will draw by hand the organisation of the facade that they are surveying. At that point, they will make a photographic portrait of the building, but always in that order. The first thing is to stop, look and observe. When the students are back in school they'll make an accurate digital drawing of what they've observed through this process of surveying. The building will then be drawn to a specific scale, and all students will draw the building they have been assigned to the same scale. And I always insist that they draw what is really there, not an idealised version of a facade. So, a satellite dish or graffiti is part of the physical character of a facade and needs to be recorded.

Another exercise I have set as a way of exploring this area of study involves asking the students to choose a domestic space they have access to, although ideally not the place they live in, and carefully photograph it to record the atmosphere of that space. They are then asked to make a model based on that photograph, normally at a scale of 1:10, that recreates the space as exactingly as possible. But this isn't the last step. The final stage of the exercise involves taking a photograph of the model, which recreates the light conditions and the atmosphere of the original space in the way that a filmmaker or even a stage-set designer would understand. What I am interested in is the image that is created through the lens of a camera at the end. I find that both these exercises help us understand more profoundly the complementary nature of our task as architects, between designing buildings and interiors for those who live in them, and adding to the built fabric of the city.

ID So, presumably, the aim of these exercises is to go beyond the generic aspects of housing and to engage with a particular place through observation.

JS That's absolutely right. Generic answers are uninteresting. I'm much more interested in students engaging with a form of investigation which is personal, but not so personal that you could never imagine it being relevant. So, the insistence is on a response that results from an attempt to understand the sum of a set of conditions that can be observed. What I always find interesting working with students is when they explore something that feels relevant rather than copying or interpreting the work we might produce in our own studio. As a teacher, it is so much more rewarding to be provoked by a work that could never be made by your own hand.

ID This takes me to another question I wanted to ask. You are officially Professor of Design and Construction. How do you teach the constructive aspect of building? How do you address the relation between a concept, a design and construction techniques?

JS You see, for me the relationship between concept and building, strategy and detail, is an inextricable one. I am not interested in a concept if there is no chance of it being realised; I'm interested in the dialogue that can exist between conceptual ambition and a real understanding of how something can be made. So, the way I teach construction is connected to the ambition of the project. When you propose a project, you should have an understanding of how you would like to build it; your ambition to create a particular atmosphere should really be grounded in an understanding of construction.

If you wanted a building to feel fragile you would know the means by which you could achieve that though construction, and if you wanted a building to feel weighty and permanent and to last for centuries, you would begin by considering how it could be built.

It starts with what kind of a building you want to build; that is the connection between strategy and detail, a concept and the way it would manifest itself in terms of construction.

ID You're teaching in Ticino, a very specific part of Switzerland – itself a very specific part of the world. I think there is a productive tension between a general teaching method and its location, and there's also a cultural tension in dealing with students of different cultures and nationalities. I was wondering whether, and to what extent, where you teach influences you and your relation with your students?

JS I've taught at so many schools… in the United Kingdom, I taught at the AA for a number of years, at ETH Zurich and EPFL in Lausanne, more recently at Harvard, Santiago de Chile and at the Milan Polytechnic. Like all of these schools, the Accademia in Mendrisio has its own particular character. But what I've come to realise is that the Accademia is a little bit like the territory of Ticino in terms of its place in Europe. Lying between the north and south of Europe, it is a place people have been passing through for thousands of years, like the design professors who converge on Mendrisio from various corners of Europe on Thursdays and Fridays… It is almost an accident that such a small city – almost in Italy, but still within Switzerland – should attract so many personalities in contemporary practice and committed teachers.

Mendrisio has that sense of being 'other', a place apart and between other places, which fosters opportunities for exchange. I hold this in very high regard; it is really one of the great qualities of the Accademia and of the small city that surrounds it. Away from the cities in which we live and work, it invites us to pause and creates the opportunity for a level of exchange and discussion, which is very particular and special. In the lives of the students, this place offers proximity to great natural beauty and very few of the distractions they would find in a big city. Life is very focused around a sense of community, which is a strong basis for developing as an architect.

ID Very nice, and very necessary. Something I think should be talked about. Going back to the notion of shared space, there is a sense in which it can be understood as a collaboration between architectural practice and teaching practice, between the structure of the office and that of the teaching studio. Can you talk a little bit about this idea of collaboration?

JS I think the task of the directors of the Venice Biennale is to create a thematic framework that is wide enough to absorb a great many different contributions and positions. In the case of Grafton Architects – Yvonne Farrell and Shelley McNamara, my colleagues at the Accademia – the theme is also closely connected to their own personality and character. I know that sharing is important to them, and I would say generosity is as well. I feel that the collaborative act of architecture is what really sets it apart from other creative disciplines. Architecture cannot exist without the complex series of collaborations on which it relies.

In my own case, collaboration started with the decision I took to work in partnership with Stephen Bates, and then, more recently, with both Stephen and Mark Tuff. We work in a studio, in fact, two studios – one in London and one in Zurich – which are open places, and the contributions from our collaborators are highly valued. In my own experience, an idea can only be developed and improved when it is tested through discussion, it is sharpened through exposure to critique, which can be gentle, as it can be challenging.

The same applies in an educational environment. I often ask students to work in pairs, and at first this may feel like an imposition, but I know that working things out requires ambition to be articulated and honed through discussion. Projects are improved through the process of critique and review, which result in better decisions than those taken autonomously. I see collaboration as a very necessary component of what it means to be an architect. And I haven't even started on the structures of collaborations that exist in the two different types of studio. In the professional studio important collaborations involve the client, consultants who contribute in numerous ways, as well as one of the messiest forms of collaboration – the act of building, which requires negotiating with the numerous people involved in the physical act of turning an idea into something concrete and physical. It's a complex business, unlike any other form of art – and that is what I profoundly enjoy about architecture.

ID Can we talk a little bit about the exhibition itself and your installation in the context of the Arsenale?

JS When Yvonne and Shelley invited the design professors at the Accademia to exhibit in Venice, I welcomed the encouragement to think about the relationship between my teaching practice and my practice as an architect. The exhibition I proposed is organised around two elements: a film by Bertie Miller and Dave Waters on my work in practice and teaching over six months, a tangible record of these two different aspects of my work and how they overlap. All the exhibits included have the same status. The film will be projected on a screen within a room created in a very delicate way, and in the middle of it, will be a table with elements produced by my students and by our practice.

ID The exhibition will take place in the very specific, very charged setting of the Arsenale. How does it respond to that setting?

JS My memory of the venue, which comes from visiting past Architecture Biennales and curating an exhibition there with Stephen Bates in 2012, is that it is quite a challenging space to exhibit in. The linear structure of the space engenders a sense of movement. And architecture is a difficult thing to exhibit, I think.

What I am attempting to do is to gently resist the walk-by character of the visits people tend to make to the Architecture Biennale by creating a room one would need to enter, which I hope will sustain their interest for a short period of time.

Zurich, 20 December 2017

Photographs by Bertie Miller

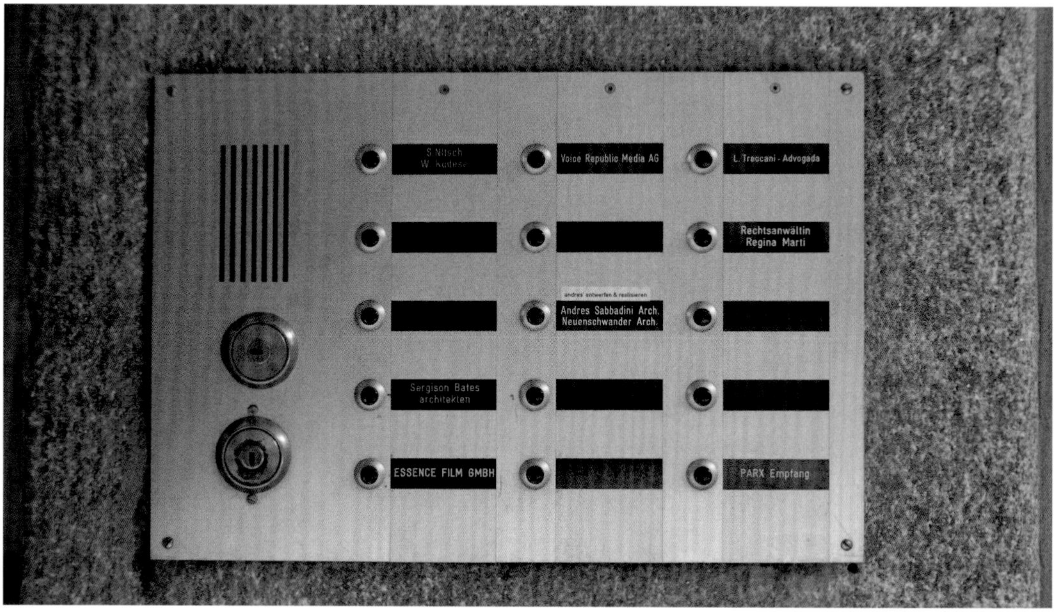
S.Nitsch
Voice Republic Media AG
L. Treccani - Advogada
Rechtsanwältin
Regina Marti
andres' entwerfen & realisieren
Andres Sabbadini Arch.
Neuenschwander Arch.
Sergison Bates
architekten
ESSENCE FILM GMBH
PARX Empfang

Ufficio
Docenti
C 3.65
Jonathan Sergison

A PLAN FOR ZURICH (1)

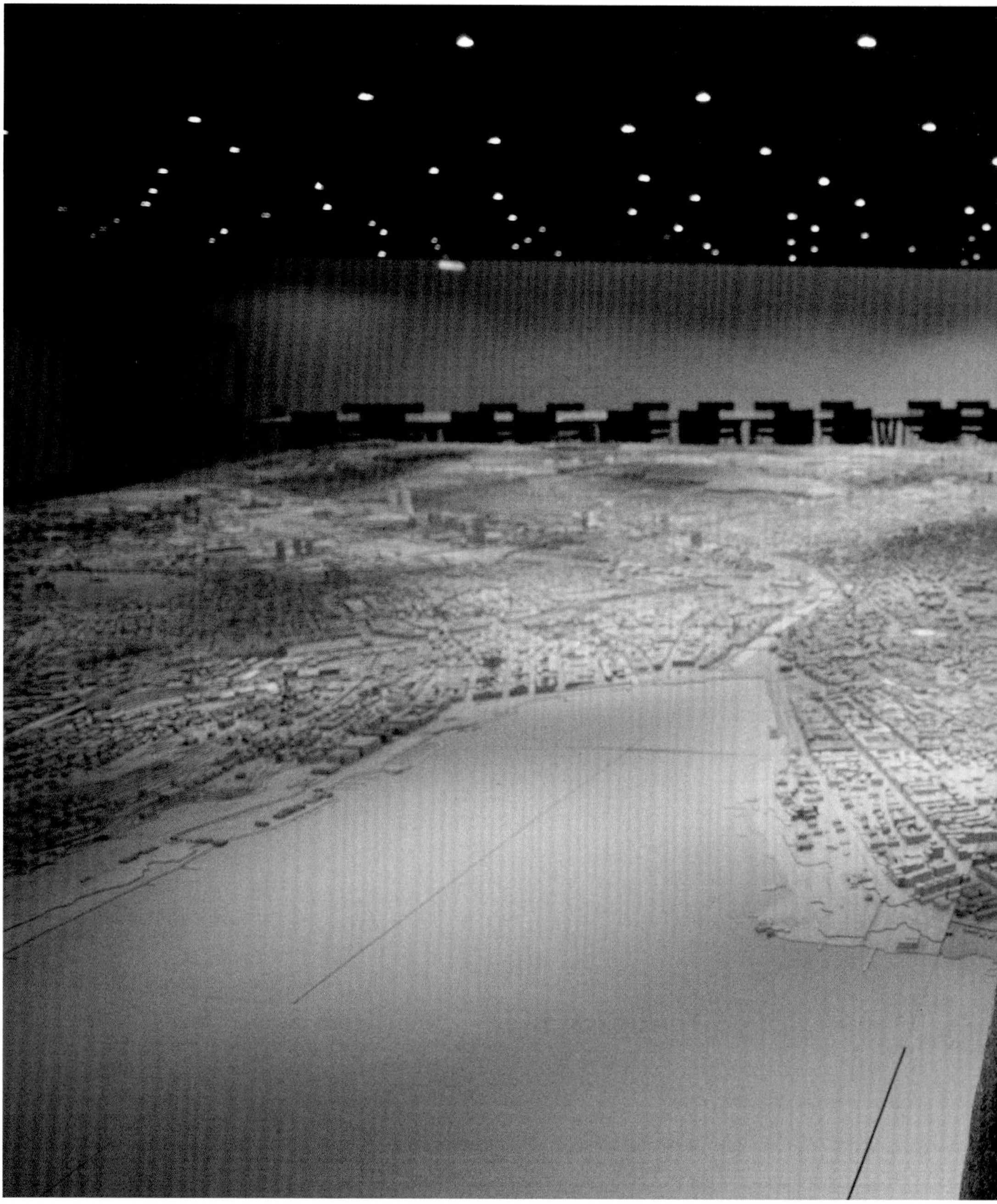

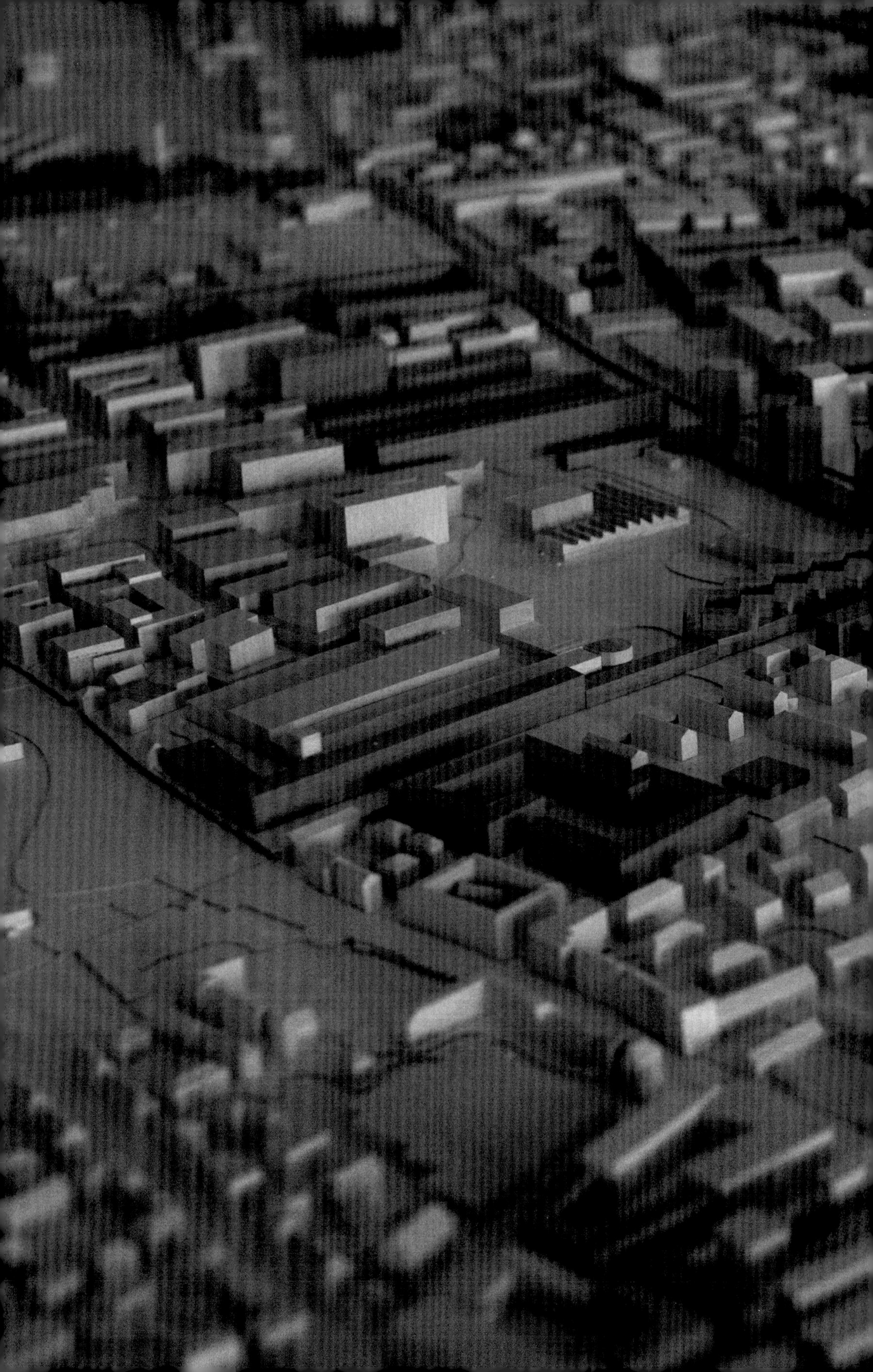

Reduce
Reuse
Recycle

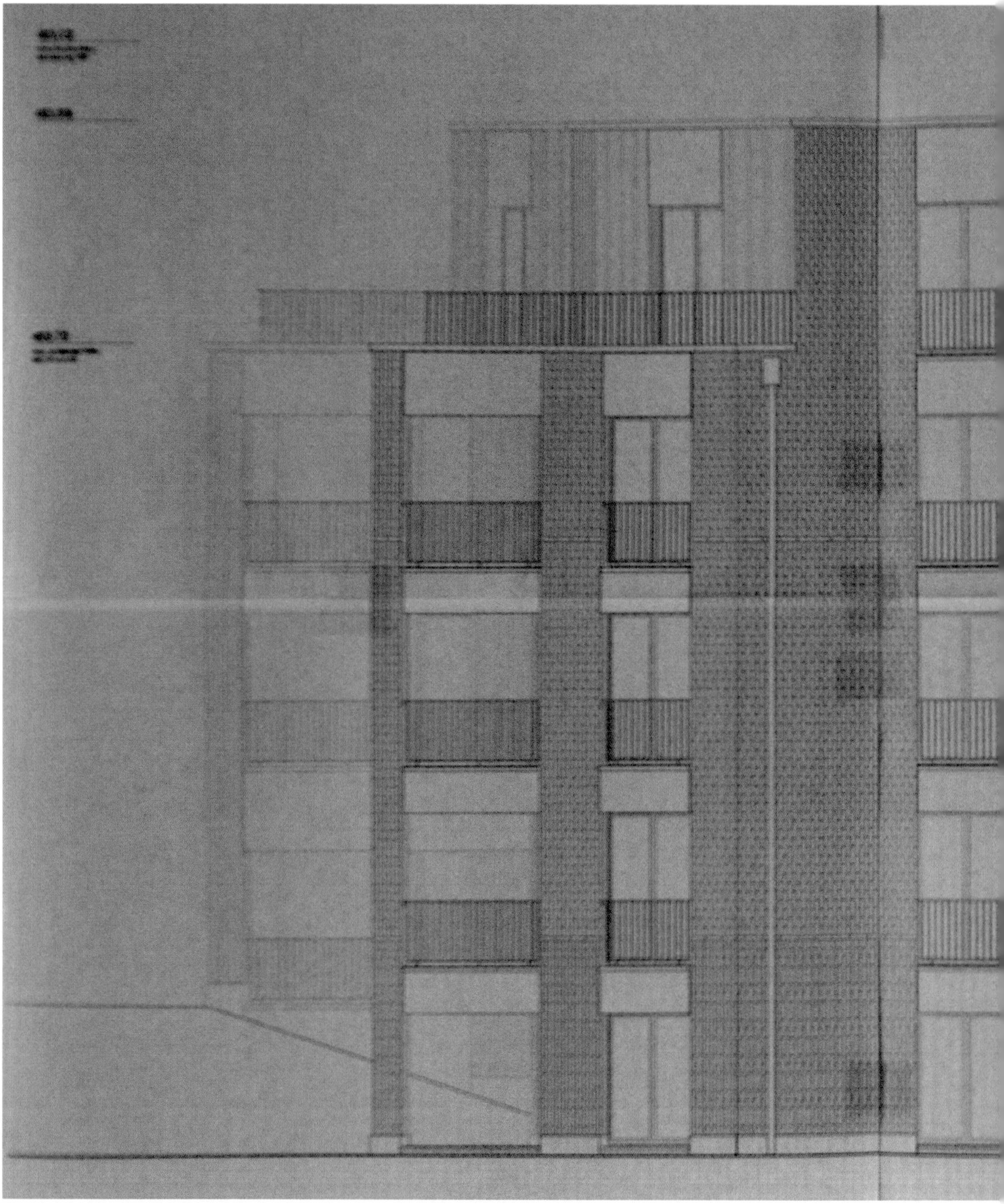

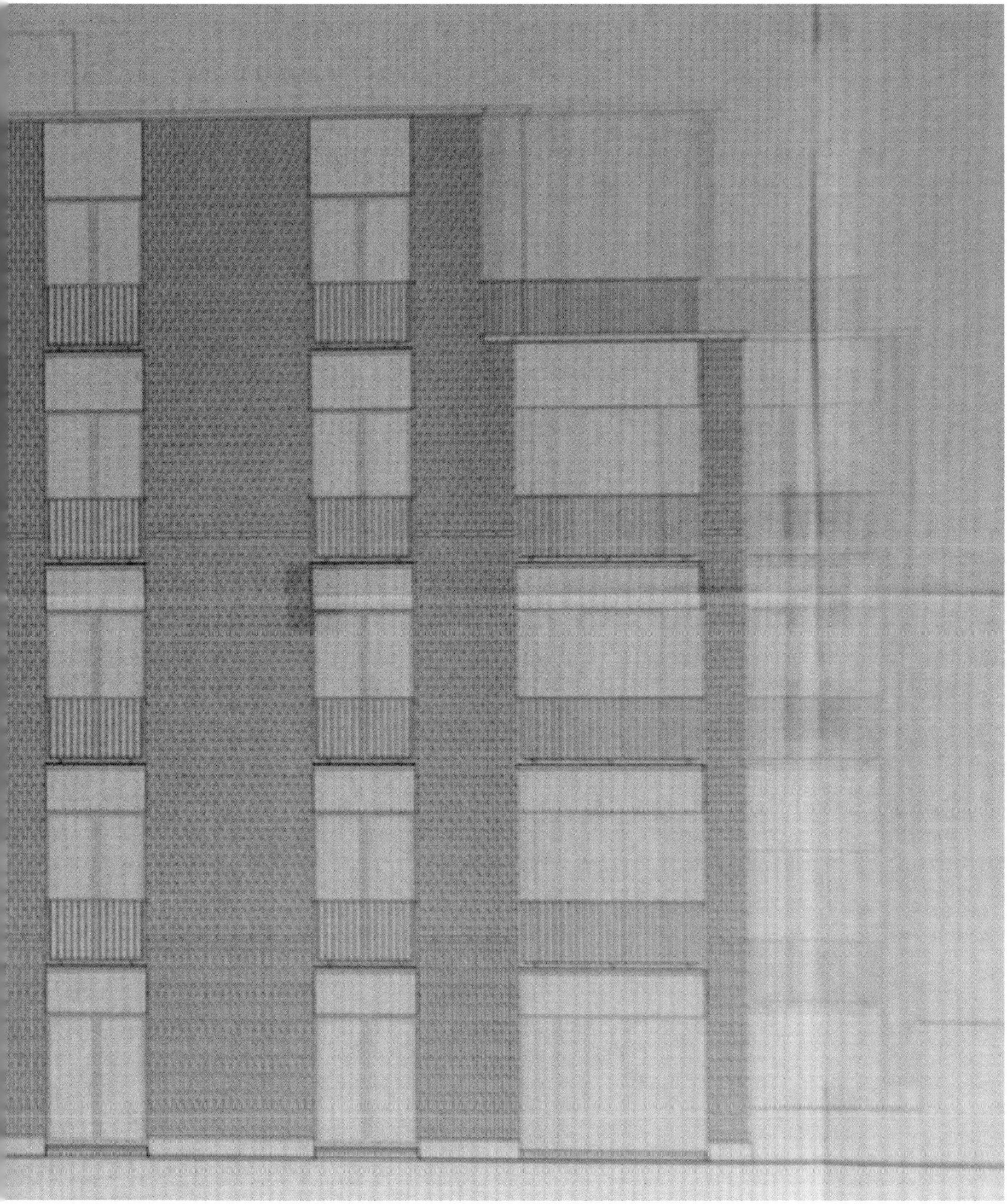

Tschopp

NON
Atelier

HEROES
DAVID GROSSMAN
SUITE FRANÇAISE
IRÈNE NÉMIROVSKY
PEREC
THE ICE
HERR DER DIEBE
A HISTORY OF THE JEWS
PAUL JOHNSON

BOB DYLAN
CLINTON HEYLIN
DYLAN & COHEN
RIMBAUD
EDMUND WHITE
INDIGNATION
PHILIP ROTH
AMOS OZ
TO THE END OF THE LAND
DAVID GROSSMAN
KAVAFIS
Philip Roth
nemesis
JOSEPH ROTH
JOB
Baudelaire
JOSE SARAMAGO
JANE GRIGSON'S
LAST WALTZ IN VIENNA
PICADOR
AMOS OZ
TO KNOW A WOMAN
HAWKSMOOR
JACOBSON
SEBASTIAN FAULKS
A YEAR
THE WILLIAM SAROYAN READER
Raymond Carver
CATHEDRAL
FIRES
MILAN KUNDERA
T.S. ELIOT
FRANCE IN THE 1980s
A HISTORY OF EUROPE SINCE 1945
TONY JUDT
Iain Sinclair
THE FOREIGNER
Clive James
North Face of Soho
The Master and Margarita
JACOBSON
Who's Sorry Now
HARUKI MURAKAMI
PHILIP ROTH
SABBATH'S THEATER
The Radetzky March

STUDIO SERGISON
Lecture by
IRINA DAVIDOVICI
RECENT SWISS ARCHITECTURE -
ORIGINS AND DEVELOPMENT
12.10.17

SHAYLOR
TARGET ZERO

Essays

I have for many years been interested in a form of practice that negotiates a position between a teaching and architectural practice. On the rare occasions I have found myself between teaching assignments, I noticed that something was lost in my contribution to practice. I found that I was not as fluent as a designer, and taking decisions seemed more laboured. As a design teacher one is compelled to form an opinion about the work of a student very quickly. This is in part the reason why I am naturally more drawn to the work of students who work in a way that is different to mine rather than derivative. They are challenging and I can learn from their work, and this is a good thing for me.

It is clear to me that my role as a teacher – I am officially professor of architectural design and construction at the Accademia in Mendrisio – is to impart to the students something of what I have learnt myself. This is knowledge that has come from years of thinking about architecture, talking about architecture and building buildings. A number of prominent London schools take a different approach and tend to hire young teachers, who are cheaper, but can only pass on a version of what they were taught themselves a few years before. This explains the anti-building culture of many of these schools, as many of their teachers have no actual experience of it.

As in professional practice, one of the biggest difficulties in the role of a teacher is making sure that your teaching practice evolves, and while the temptation is to repeat exercises, it is important to resist this.

What abilities should students have after studying architecture?

When I finished my studies at the AA in London in 1989, I was not really ready to make a meaningful contribution to architectural practice. I could draw by hand reasonably well. I knew a little bit about twentieth-century architecture – although on a more or less self-taught basis – and very little of the much broader history of architecture. And I knew very little about construction – I had studied at the AA, after all.

The burden of teaching me what would make me useful to practice was shouldered by the offices I had the good fortune to work in, and the longer the interval between my architectural education and professional activities grows, the more certain I am that this is not a good thing. In the UK, and especially in many London schools, there is much emphasis on a sort of liberal and undisciplined form of experimentation, and not enough attention is given to what I would call solid architectural knowledge. Worse than this, many UK graduates have to unlearn what they have been taught at school before they can begin to be useful. For many, the experience of entering the workplace leads to a great sense of disappointment.

I could take this point further and tell you that architects educated in the UK are a rarity in our London studio and, thinking about it, I would not offer a position in our studio to the person I was when I finished my studies. This sounds a bit like the Groucho Marx quip about not wanting to be a member of a club that would have me, but there is a more serious point here.

I do not believe that it is realistic to expect students to be fully formed architects ready to face any challenge when they finish their studies. We all know that the training of an architect takes many years of work and the accumulation of much experience. In the UK you need to undergo a rather arduous further training after completing your diploma course, and it is the obtaining of this additional qualification that allows qualified architects to practise legally.

One of the greatest bits of good fortune I had was to emerge from architectural school at a time when there was not very much work. This might sound paradoxical, but the lack of work offered me time to invest in theoretical speculation and in time to develop a critical framework of friends and collaborators, many of whom are today rather well-known architects. In the early 1990s we had time to think and meet and discuss architecture. If there had been an abundance of work, this would probably not have happened.

Recent graduates from Swiss schools of architecture are emerging into a work place that is so different to the one I faced back in 1989. Schools in Switzerland are very well structured and their staff include many exceptional teachers who are often very talented architects in practice. Graduates of the *Fachhochschulen*, ETH Zurich or EPFL are likely to be technically capable even if they have limited experience of applying their knowledge. And they most certainly have been exposed to some very good architecture – because it is all around them.

If anything, the problem is arguably that this is too much of a good thing. There is a lot of work in Switzerland, and many very good offices to work in.

But the question I am really interested in is what the best model of practice is today. What skills do architects need when they finish their education? I know the form of practice I am involved in is rather old-fashioned. We were lucky to be able to build enough in our first years in practice to be able to demonstrate a certain competence that then allowed us to build more, because the criteria used to determine eligibility in many competitions require competitors to have experience of building, and it is through competitions that we have won the vast majority of our work. But this does not really help young architects today: they have to enter open competitions where the odds are stacked against them. Each new issue of *Hochparterre Wettbewerbe* introduces me to another new young Swiss office and I ask myself what they will do to add to the culture of architecture in Switzerland.

The further away architects are drawn from a solid grounding in useful knowledge, the less relevant they become. I know it is easier and more fun to do the pseudo-experimental nonsense that goes on in certain London and many North American schools, but it does not really help graduates and it does not make good architecture. So, I hope that Swiss schools can continue to organise the education of architects in the way they have for many years and resist introducing change just because it is seen as more interesting. There is too much at stake, and too much to lose.

The Accademia di Architettura in Mendrisio, the school I teach in, is a very young school and it is exciting to be involved in the process of organising ways of doing things, and establishing procedures for the first time. But we are looking very carefully at what works and what does not. In some ways, it reminds me of our discussions when we were setting up in practice. We know that our school cannot compete with ETH and EPFL in terms of technical research, and nor should it. The school has attracted some very strong personalities to teach design, and urban issues are given a degree of priority. It is clear to many of us that we will increasingly work in urban situations, prevalently in the European cities we have inherited, rather than building new cities. All the design studios in Mendrisio have their own critical position and offer a level of experimentation, but we all believe that the art of architecture lies in building, although we explore this in different ways. There is a lot of respect and a lot of exchange, and the geographical remoteness of the school is a positive quality as it offers teachers and students a retreat and little distraction.

So what skills do I think an architect should have when they complete their studies? There are many that would never be listed in a course curriculum: curiosity, humility, a sense of social responsibility, a thick skin, the ability to remain optimistic and manage disappointment, the ability to manage money, recognising that originality comes through years of hard work and a commitment to the discipline of architecture, not the desire to be original for its own sake. More concretely: the ability to think conceptually, to work collaboratively, the building blocks of a critical position, a basic knowledge of the principles of construction, some knowledge and an interest in the history of architecture, the ability to look at things and understand what you see.

I think it would be helpful for some graduates to be reminded that it takes a long time to gain command of the discipline of architecture: there are no short cuts, and learning from good architects is better than trying to teach yourself.

First given as a presentation at the Symposium on Architectural Education held at the Lucerne University of Applied Sciences on 4 March 2016

Transcript published in: *Architekturpädagogiken, Hochschule Luzern – Technik & Architektur*, Institut für Architektur and Park Books AG, Zurich 2017, 217–222

A number of years ago we were invited to take part in a competition for a housing project in north London. At some point in the competitive interview I stated that every project we undertake is unique in the set of interests it investigates, and could be understood as a form of research. I still believe that this is true, although I would be cautious about making the same comment again in such circumstances. We did not win the competition and found out later that a number of members of the members of the jury took issue with my statement. They misconstrued it, thinking that what we had in mind was some form of speculative enterprise with implicit risks and an uncertain outcome, which they would be funding. I now understand the difficulty the client had. Naturally, they wanted to be assured that we had the experience and competence to deliver a building that would serve their needs and be fit for purpose.

When we set up in practice, Stephen Bates and I had learnt some things about building from working for a number of established architects in practice. We accepted a future of uncertainty, although this was countered by great optimism on our part. Looking back, it is clear that a series of events that were wholly out of our control have shaped the practice we now have. Many of the projects we dealt with in the early years we did for the first time, and this partly explains why it feels that we did more research then than we do now. I do, however, believe that we are constantly building upon a set of shared interests, and while the knowledge we have acquired through building is cumulative, our restless curiosity to explore new themes and ideas remains unchanged.

Reflecting on our twenty-one years in practice, I can identify a number of lessons we have learnt by engaging with the challenges posed by different projects at various times. Here, I have chosen twenty-one of them as examples of what amounts to a form of research in practice.

1. Breathing wall construction

In 1997 we won a national competition to design a contemporary version of the ubiquitous semi-detached house or double house. This building type is associated with the suburban expansion of many towns and cities in the UK: approximately three million of them were built in the 1920s and 1930s, and today they are the most common housing type in the UK, accounting for 32 percent of housing stock.

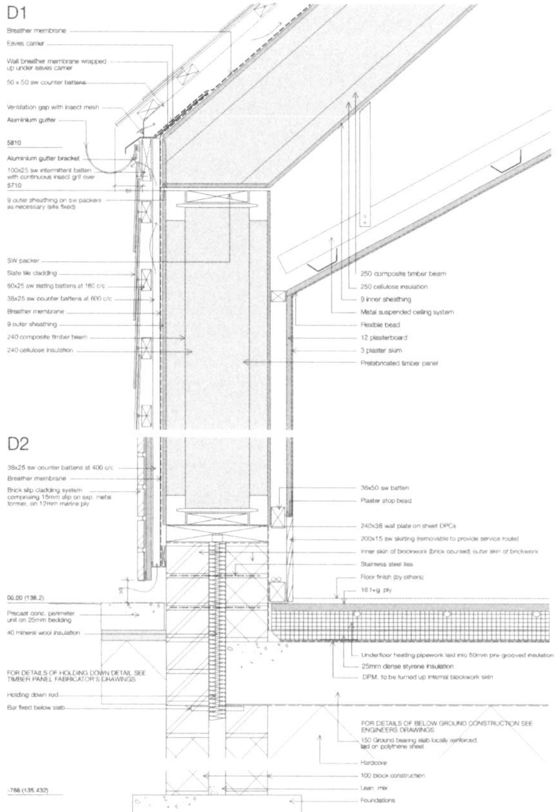

One aspect of our reflection on this topic was to consider what form of construction could be employed in volume house building. We investigated thoroughly the possibilities of timber panel construction with the obvious benefits of prefabrication in speeding up site construction and for quality control. But we were also interested in exploring breathing wall construction and sought a form of building where air could pass from the inside to the outside of a house without compromising its thermal properties or water tightness. It is widely known that pollution levels inside homes contribute to poor health. On completion, the project was monitored for a year, at the end of which the residents reported the houses to be easy to heat and air quality significantly better than in previous accommodation. One resident who suffered from asthma had had no attacks over the period. We have subsequently employed timber panel construction on a number of other projects.

2. A range of ironmongery

In 2005 we developed an ironmongery range for izé. We wanted to find better versions of the elements and fittings we specify in our projects: window catches, trickle vents, sash locks, door and window handles, amongst others. The process of developing and prototyping was lengthy and we learnt that adjustments of less than a millimetre would affect the proportion and appearance of the elements we developed. This taught us a lot about the properties of materials and how they weather.

3. Teaching and practice

I have been actively involved in teaching architecture for more than twenty-five years. The relationship between teaching and practice is an important one: teaching affords me the opportunity to explore themes and issues that relate to practice, but with greater freedom. Combining practice and teaching benefits both.

In my teaching I tend to prioritise urban issues and housing projects. Over the coming semesters my students at the Accademia in Mendrisio will be working on a development plan for the city of Zurich. This project will be undertaken over three years and in each semester we will be working in different areas of the city to develop strategies for movement, public realm, work places, public buildings, housing and to assess the status of buildings that are currently protected in some form. The urban planning and development department of the city of Zurich is a partner in this work and we will be working in collaboration with architects, critics and urban thinkers. The city is currently committed to a programme of building to house a growing population within the existing urban territory. Every student is studying a neighbourhood or city block in detail to develop concrete proposals. The sum of our work over six semesters will offer concrete proposals for Zurich. As on many occasions in the past, the studio is engaging in a form of research that goes beyond the coursework requirements.

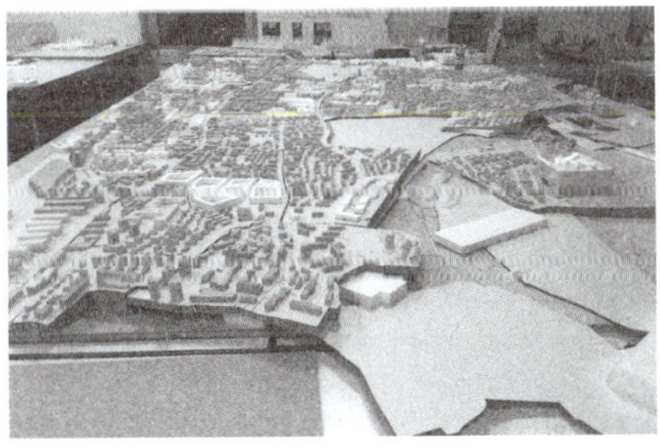

4. A door detail

When we first started visiting Switzerland, we came across a door hinge that was not known to us. It enables a door to be detailed in a way that overlaps with the frame, and therefore enables one to place these two elements on the outer or inner face of a wall, rather than in between. Furthermore this type of hinge can be adjusted to ensure that the door does not catch on the floor. This is one of countless examples of a simple and practical application of building construction techniques observed in Switzerland and adapted to our own projects in the Zurich studio. However, it is important to note that small differences in ways of building are not always transferable. A UK carpenter would not be familiar with this type of hinge and might struggle to fix it.

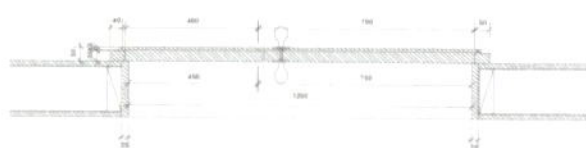

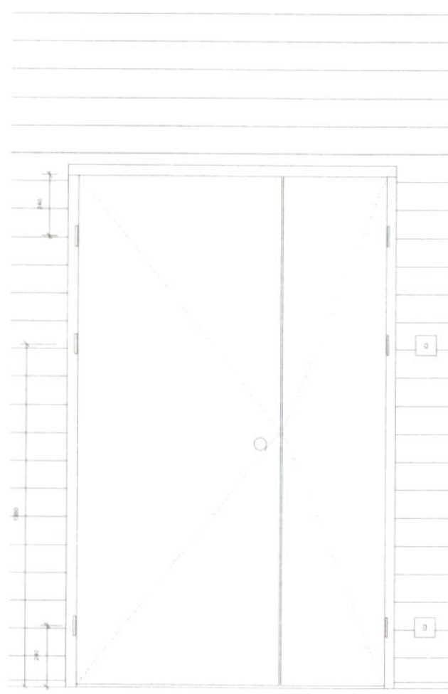

5. Papers

I have already acknowledged the importance of the relationship between practice and teaching, but writing is another form of practice that mediates between these two concerns. As a whole these form overlapping and complementary disciplines.
To date Stephen Bates and I have published three collections of illustrated essays. Many of them relate to the themes we are

exploring with our students, or to invitations to lecture on specific subjects. While neither of us would claim that they are necessarily academic, our shared interests and commitment to writing stems from the fact that it helps us articulate and make sense of what we are working on, and from the desire to share these reflections with each other – and eventually with a wider readership.

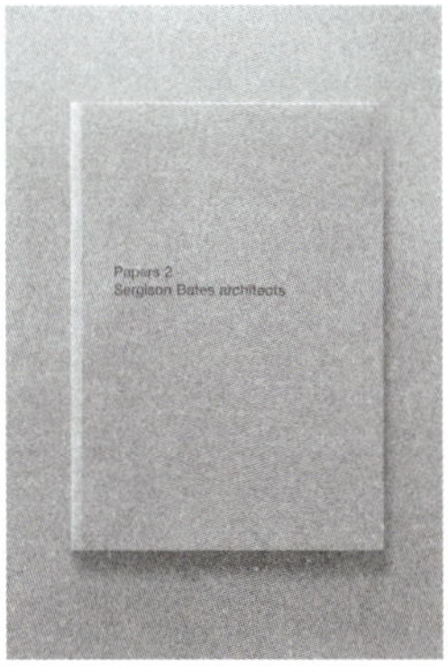

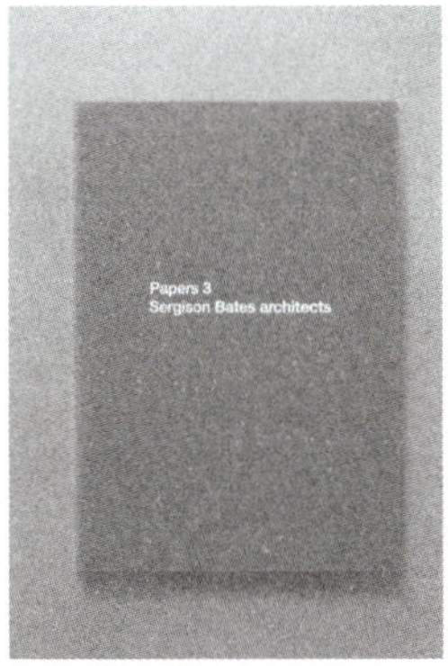

6. Concrete panel construction

Working in collaboration with Geneva-based architect Jean-Paul Jaccaud, we were able to learn from the wonderful precast concrete industry in the west of Switzerland for the project we won in competition in 2006. A number of concrete factories have been active in this part of the country since the 1950s and 1960s and have considerable experience in this form of construction. For the building we realised on Rue du Cendrier, in an old inner city quarter of Geneva, we developed a system of L- and T-shaped elements that, when assembled, give the impression of a tectonic framed building. The individual pieces have an inner structural concrete layer, a thick middle layer of insulation and an outer layer of 'decorative' concrete. The elements were complex in terms of their geometries and were fabricated extremely accurately. The outer finish of the panels is intentionally different and explores four different colours as a way of evoking the subtle differences that exist in the local stone.

7. Brickwork as a rain screen

For the Studio house in Bethnal Green, in east London, we wanted a facade that would not explicitly have a 'house-like' appearance, as the house was also used as a place of work. The intention was to create a series of horizontal elements in the facade, where the windows are stretched across the width of the street elevation with alternating brick layers. This was favoured over a brick surface with punched openings. The building is constructed from a lightweight timber frame and to reduce the load imposed on the structure we elected to use thin brick slips, which were prebonded onto cementitious boards, one brick course high. The panels interlock and the process of building was closer to carpentry then to brick construction. We did, however, point the joints and apply mortar slurry to the outer surface.

8. The restoration of Upper Lawn

One of the numerous invisible adjustments we made to this seminal house by Alison and Peter Smithson involved the introduction of underfloor heating. Two layers of pipes were placed in the void between the ceiling of the ground floor and the floor above. Radiant heat is provided by hot water running in plastic pipes, which offers the building a degree of background heat and ensures a stable temperature in the winter months.

D1

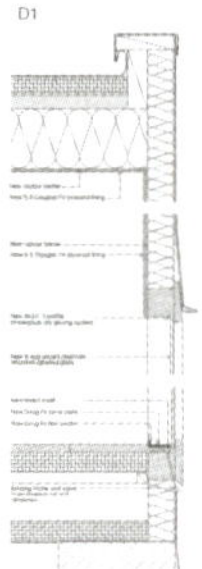

D2

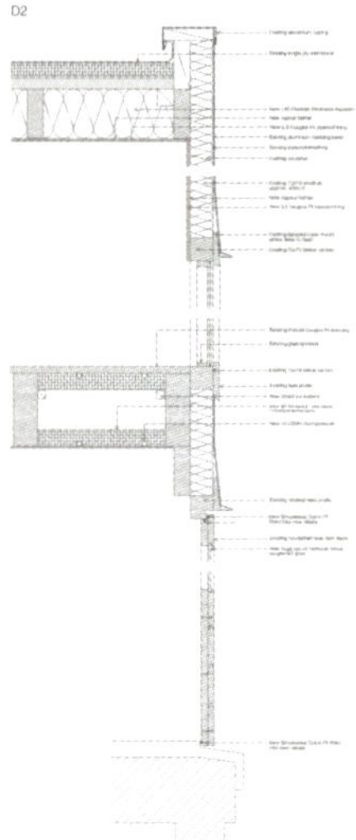

9. A brick building in Zurich

While it is not widely used as a building material in contemporary construction, in the nineteenth and early twentieth centuries much of the built fabric of Zurich employed brick as a masonry element that was subsequently covered in render. Where brickwork is on display in these older buildings, a light beige or red brick was used. In the two apartment buildings we are currently constructing in Zurich we are employing a system of vertically aligned brick slips. We are drawing upon the experience we have acquired from building in the UK, and more recently in Belgium. The bricks we are using in this project are sourced in Belgium, where the widest choice of good quality bricks is available at economically advantageous prices.

10. A poured rubber floor

In 2002 we were invited to refurbish an apartment on the thirty-fourth floor of one of the towers in the Barbican complex in the City of London. One issue that preoccupied us was finding a floor finish that would seem appropriate for this Brutalist building. We considered linoleum, but were concerned about the joints and its general utilitarian feel. After a lengthy process of research we contacted a company that specialises in poured rubber floors. We found this to be suitably abstract, and it was poured through all of the rooms in one single process. This floor finish is generally used in large factory floors and industrial facilities. After we published the project, we received numerous calls from architects requesting details of the company we used.

11. Open brick joints

The timber panel construction system we developed for the semi-detached housing project in Stevenage was also used in an urban housing project in north London we won in competition in 1999. In this project we were interested in giving expression to the breathing wall aspect of the panels and elected to create a matrix of open vertical joints at regular intervals. We noticed people would stop in the street to look at the building and heard anecdotally that one interested party thought that these gaps were left by the removal of the scaffolding, as in mediaeval Italian buildings. While the reality is more prosaic, we were happy with the subtle grid it created on the facades and with the interest it aroused.

12. An internal corridor with open courtyards

In contemporary housing projects in the UK developers often put pressure on architects to employ internal central corridors with apartments on either side. This is because a core can serve many dwellings and allows a deeper section, which ensures that the form is more efficient. In 1999 we were invited to add a floor of apartments to an existing three-storey former industrial building in Wandsworth, London. A part of this building was so deep in plan that we needed to consider an internal corridor, although in this instance we were able to arrange the apartments with an entrance yard which is open to the sky. Timber gates were constructed which met neither the floor nor the ceiling, allowing light to be brought into the central circulation space. We were happy with the result of the set of decisions we took, but of course this solution is only applicable to top floors or single-storey buildings.

13. In-situ concrete

The fields surrounding this new house in Hampshire are strewn with large flints that are revealed when they are ploughed. Flint is sometimes used as a facing material on the walls of buildings in this region: the cut face of the stone has a scale-like appearance, but the material is sharp and very durable. Through a lengthy process of testing we investigated ways of using flints as an aggregate in the construction of in-situ concrete walls. The cut face would be carefully placed in the shuttering and would then be revealed in the struck concrete. The process of casting needs to take account of the reach of an arm and therefore the process of building will be slow and determined by reach. On completion the outer concrete surface will be hammered to reveal the aggregate, creating a rough surface.

14. Tilt-up concrete panel construction

This form of construction is commonly used in the building of warehouses and industrial buildings in North America. One face of the panel is cast onto the concrete floor slab. It is a direct and rather pragmatic way of forming large panels of concrete on site, so that they do not need to be transported from another location, but simply craned into position. We drew upon this form of construction for the wall panels of the applied art centre we built in north Wales. In this instance, the panels were formed from an inner structural layer of concrete cast on the slab, an inner layer of rigid insulation and an outer layer that is pigmented and combed vertically in predetermined areas. The panels were then lifted into position and propped until the roof secured them. At that moment the building appeared like a stage set.

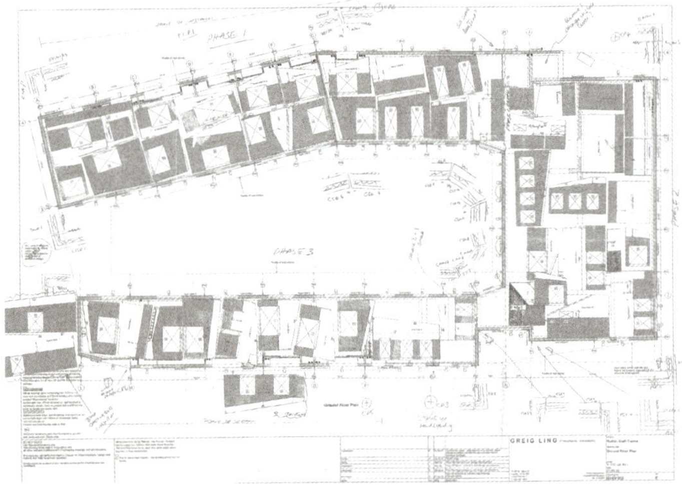

15. Tiles

We have found ourselves employing encaustic tiles on a number of projects in recent years. For a recent care home project in Belgium we worked with Benoît van Innis, who created a range of hand-painted tiles, which were applied as decorative elements around the windows. The tiles create a subtle expression of domesticity, framing windows like curtains: their pattern combinations provide variety and lend a familiar character to the building, contributing to reduce the visual impact of its scale.

16. Colour

In a number of projects we have experimented with bolder colours. I am not sure that we have been totally satisfied with the results: we tend to favour colours that are earthy, muted, quite sober. Where it feels appropriate the colours of the materials we use are expressed or gently adjusted by applying stains and paint washes. We give considerable attention to the finishing of materials and often experiment to test different solutions. Finishing is the last process in building and it is wholly reliant on the skill of those on site.

17. A tiled corner

When we were working on the semi-detached housing project in Stevenage, we devoted a considerable amount of time to studying the setting out of the Eternit tiles, particularly the horizontal coursing. Eventually Mark Tuff built a model at 1:5, which enabled us to understand this issue. Later the model was taken to site and left as a tangible indicator of what we wanted to achieve. Finding the right balance between being demanding with construction and taking time to make the right decision is very important. A willingness to engage with this process on the part of the subcontractors on site is also necessary, but increasingly rare.

18. Furniture

For many years we have been interested in designing furniture. The first items we designed predate the time we formally established our practice. I have a great interest in furniture and the relationship between comfort, proportion and the assembly of elements. We are currently developing a range of furniture for Soeder, a Zurich-based company, and unlike the bespoke items we developed in the past, this range is intended for mass production and a wider market.

19. Bespoke doors and windows

In many of our early projects we were dissatisfied with the door and window systems we found in the building industry and, where possible, preferred to produce bespoke elements to control the proportions of the elements and sightlines. In the Wandsworth project I described above, the apartments were sold on the open market. This meant that to meet the mortgage requirements of future owners, the doors and windows needed to conform to rigorous standards of air and water tightness. The main contractor also had a joinery workshop and our client was willing to support our ambition to develop special windows for this project. I remember our associate frequently having to visit a test centre to propose various refinements, until the windows satisfied the standards. This happened a long time ago and, on reflection, it seems rather self-indulgent on our part. Since then we have used existing, widely available window systems and worked with the constraints they impose.

20. Recessed lighting tubes

One of our earliest projects involved the remodelling and refurbishment of a former pub into the studio of our long-standing friends and collaborators, graphic designers Cartlidge Levene. Many aspects of this project involved developing a way of building that we had no previous experience of. One decision that comes to mind was the recessing of the metal box of fluorescent light fittings to reveal only the lighting elements. While it was a little fiddly for the contractor to neatly build a series of pockets in the plasterboard walls and ceilings, I still enjoy the result: it transforms an ordinary element, the ubiquitous fluorescent light fitting, into something more refined.

21. Ornamental brickwork

Over the years, working increasingly farther afield, we find ourselves returning time and time again to the possibilities of one of the most primitive building materials: the simple brick. While we would never impose brick construction on a local building industry that has no experience of using it, for one reason or another we tend to work in places where there is a long-standing tradition of brickwork. For our soon-to-be-completed housing project in Hampstead, north London, we were fascinated with the fine neighbouring Arts and Crafts buildings from the end of the nineteenth century and their ornamental brickwork.

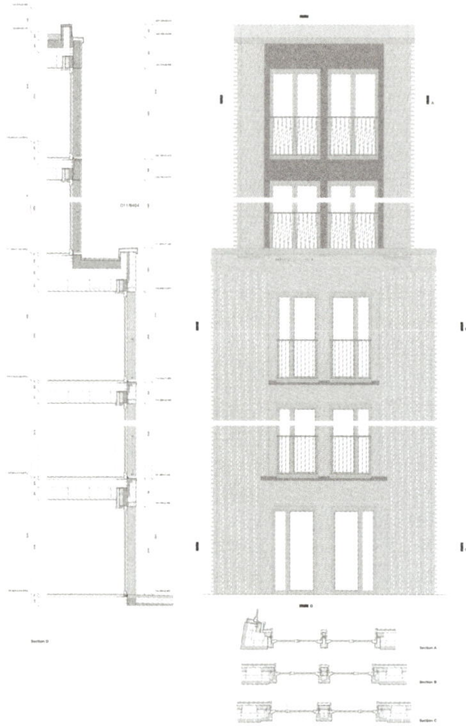

While the circumstances in which these older buildings were realised are far removed from today's, we would argue that it is possible, within the constraints of contemporary construction, to build in brick in a way that is more than merely expedient or functional.

While the points I have made about our various projects are anecdotal and none of what we have built would exist without the lessons and inspiration we have found in the work of others, this documents a continuous search for a way of building that serves conceptual ambitions. Sometimes answers are found in surprising places, and the journey any project follows from inception to completion is always uncertain. The idea of research is often overstated in architecture, but I do like the 'search' that lies within the word 'research'. Searching for interesting ways of using ordinary things is a large part of what we do.

A version of this text was first published in *arq*, vol. 21, no. 4, 2017, 298–309

The legacy of Brutalism was already part of the urban landscape of London in the 1970s, as I was growing up. On weekends, I would cross Waterloo Bridge and pass the National Theatre by Denys Lasdun. When I was older, my parents often took me there, and found the interior spaces impressive, almost cathedral-like. I remember visiting the Barbican before it was open to the public with my father, who was an engineer. I had never encountered a building of such complexity and scale.

When I began my formal education as an architect I was taught by Adrian Sanson, a member of the Grunt Group. In my year out I met Neave Brown, and later still Patrick Hodgkinson. Both left a strong impression on me. Their approach seemed rooted in a post-war belief that architecture could deliver the changes society needed. They were uncompromising, and like others of their generation their political conviction went beyond the need to rebuild and construct at an unprecedented scale. This touched me, although I cannot say that I ever shared their conviction, largely because I was exposed to the growing hostility the post-war welfare state building programme was attracting in the 1980s.

In the second and third year of my degree course, I was affected by the revaluation of pre-modern architecture in the work of James Stirling and James Gowan, among others at the time. In my last two years at the Architectural Association School of Architecture in London, any interest in Postmodernism was dismissed, and I found myself looking with renewed interest at modern architecture, and more specifically at post-war English examples. The Brunswick Centre by Patrick Hodgkinson, the National Theatre, the Royal College of Physicians, the SOAS library and the College of Education by Denys Lasdun are all in the area of London I lived in. Later still, I got to know James Stirling's buildings in Oxford and Cambridge, and found them intriguing. Kettle's Yard in Cambridge and Middleton Hall at the University of Hull by Lesley Martin, The Lawns halls of residence, also in Hull, by Gillespie, Kidd & Coia present a northern European Modernism and, like the later buildings by Lewerentz, employ brick, concrete, timber and copper. I still find them extremely powerful.

Several years after I finished my studies, I became interested in the work Alison and Peter Smithson. When I did meet them, I found them quite intriguing: they expressed little sense of doubt, and their reputation for grumpiness and arrogance was well earned, although I did not find it off-putting. Three projects, all houses, remain a strong source of reference for me today.

The first, the Upper Lawn Pavilion in Fonthill, Wiltshire, is particularly significant because in 2004 we had the good fortune to restore it for its current owners, Ian and Jo Cartlidge. They should be credited for saving the garden of the house, a project that the Smithsons described as the embodiment of the Brutalist landscape. Having the opportunity to take the building apart, which was made necessary by the condition it was in forty years after it was constructed, we developed a better insight into the notion of strategy and detail. In the same way one understands a machine by taking it apart, we became intimately aware of an attitude in the Smithsons' approach to exploring detailing.

I visited the second house, the Sugden House in Watford, in 1994. This project helped me understand the concepts of 'the everyday' and 'the ordinary'. These themes and concepts were extremely helpful when we set up in practice in 1996. In the context of the conservative planning regulations of the 1990s, we hoped that couching our conceptual ambitions in forms that may be read as normal and familiar would help us win planning consent.

The third house I remember studying carefully was the Smithson's unbuilt project for a home and studio on Colville Place in Soho, London. They referred to this project as the first example of New Brutalism and described it as a 'warehouse' model. Its scale and organisation suggest an interpretation of the English terraced house, although I am sure the Smithsons would not approve of this comparison.

The other project by the Smithsons I find myself returning to time and time again is The Economist assembly of buildings in Mayfair, Central London, which is a great urban work at many levels. It seems indebted to the lessons the Smithsons must have learnt visiting the great North American cities. But to Raynor Banham, who takes credit for coining the term 'New Brutalism', The Economist building represents the end of the Smithsons' connection with this movement in architecture.

I also find myself returning to Denys Lasdun. Nearly every day for fifteen years I walked past the end of the College of Education building in Bloomsbury. In time, I came to realise that if we disregards the service towers, which I do not care for, the scale of the building, its length, height and tonality are remarkably similar to that of the neighbouring terraced streets. The northeast corner sets up an explicit relationship with the Thomas Cubitt terrace that sits across the street from it. I do not know how intentional this was, and whether Lasdun was even aware of it, but I do find it instructive, for it references an older tradition of building in the same way that the use of certain building materials establishes a connection with existing building traditions.

These examples of English Brutalism may be of a place and time that no longer exists; nevertheless, I find they are still relevant – not as examples of a style, but certainly in terms of their social and conceptual ambition.

First presented at Finding Brutalism in Great Britain, a symposium held at the Lucerne University of Applied Sciences, 19 October 2017

Contemporary architecture has an inextricable link to the notion of re-use. At this moment in history, all our activities as architects working in western Europe depend on understanding and negotiating a relationship with the cumulative results of the activities of the past on the landscape we inhabit and the urban conditions we are surrounded by – in other words, the world 'as found'. As Peter Smithson once stated, "'as found' is a simple affair, it is about being careful".[1] In this sense, carefulness can be equated with understanding, studying the object in question in depth. In Smithson's words, 'the art is in the picking up, turning over and putting with…'[2]

The most logical way of organising the study of something that exists is to carry out a survey, looking carefully and recording through photographs and accurately scaled drawings the object of study. The art of surveying has a long tradition and clearly determined set of conventions that allow us to understand and share information. In the Renaissance studies were made of classical antiquities, and in North America pioneers were commissioned to produce land surveys as a way of understanding the nature of the territory of the 'New World'. In this sense surveying must precede re-use, as it informs our understanding of what already exists.

As an architect, most of my work takes place in European cities, which have developed over the centuries, often through the rebuilding and adjusting of Greek or Roman foundations. In this role, it is necessary to develop a relationship to our urban heritage and to the myriad ways in which cities have been shaped by the past. We live in a time and place where it is highly unlikely that we will be charged with the task of building an entirely new city, even though we may be involved in projects of considerable scale. We also live in a time when buildings and whole neighbourhoods are increasingly protected by planning laws, and different agencies regulate the use and preservation of our built heritage. At times it seems that the historical centre of some cities are museums of buildings. Numerous Italian cities come to mind: Venice is an extreme example, a city that was 'completed' many centuries ago and is now in a state of gradual ruin and decay, a mere object of tourist consumption. In this case, there is little opportunity to effect change and, as architects, our role is reduced to preserving the existing urban fabric. Of course, this is in itself not without interest or intellectual challenge.

What type of paint should be used to redecorate building when the original paint types are no longer produced? How should we replace a window when the original falls well short of contemporary energy standards but has such elegant proportions? Is it appropriate to fit a contemporary heating system in a house that was previously cooled by passive means and heated

1 Thomas Schregenberger, "'As found' is a Small Affair", in *Architecture Is Not Made With the Brain: The Labour of Alison and Peter Smithson*, Architectural Association, London 2005, 83

2 Claude Lichtenstein and Thomas Schregenberger (eds.), *As Found: The Discovery of the Ordinary*, Lars Müller Publishers, Zurich 2001, 40

by wood-burning fireplaces? These are just a few of the numerous questions one is compelled to address when restoring an old building. It is a task that results in impure solutions, though not necessarily inappropriate or unintelligent ones. In a country like Italy, the need to preserve a rich and highly significant building heritage creates an enormous burden on financial resources.

In addition to the cultural aspects associated with the re-use of buildings, we also need to take into account the environmental imperative. An existing building contains embodied energy and by extending the life of any edifice we are mitigating its initial environmental impact. While it is invariably more financially advantageous to demolish and rebuild an existing structure, materials have to be disposed of, and any new building will have some form of environmental impact.

Finally, re-use needs to be understood more widely in relation to culture, and to the enormous body of ideas and inventions that shape all aspects of contemporary life, as it has an inextricable connection to existing knowledge. In the past, creative practice always drew upon older, seminal models: priority was given to studying the existing, and interpretation followed, always in that order. While it may be tempting to believe that invention does not require an understanding of history, it is both arrogant and futile to think that the past has no bearing on the present. Drawing upon the cultural achievements of the past and investing in understanding them fully is a much more constructive way of approaching our work as architects.

First given as an introduction to a lecture at MantovArchitettura, 25 May 2017

> (…) Urban architecture needs only to look back on its own tradition. The antique city, that of the Middle Ages and of the Renaissance, that of the Baroque and Neoclassical periods, and also that of the nineteenth and twentieth centuries, followed formal convention that was perceived not as a burden but quite the opposite: as a canon of beauty and privilege. Residing behind the regular facades of Siena, Florence, London or Paris were not oppressed persons or conformists, but rather a motley assortment of citizens of differing provenance and personality. The canon to which they voluntarily submitted when building (which was zealously guarded by their communities) did not attest to a lack of character; it was a sign of shared responsibility and community pride.[1]

1 Vittorio Magnago Lampugnani, 'The Individual, Society, and the Architecture of the City' in: *And Now the Ensemble!!!*, Miroslav Šik and the Swiss Arts Council Pro Helvetia (eds.), Lars Müller Publishers, Zurich, 2012, 25

The case Lampugnani makes rather forcefully is for a contemporary architecture that considers continuity, respects and validates an older tradition of city building and urbanism. I find myself agreeing wholeheartedly with his radical call to order which invites architects to consider their role and responsibility, and be guided by a sense of urban decorum and good manners, rather than by the desire for uniqueness and spectacle.

My fascination with the European city began with London, although – like most people who consider themselves Londoners – I was not born there. My first memories of cities are of Chester and Liverpool, in the north-west of England. Chester is a Roman city, and this may explain my fascination with the Roman urban concept that left such an indelible mark on it, as on many others throughout Europe and north Africa. In Chester, the *decumanus* and *cardo* are still clearly legible, the fortifying walls are still intact and some remarkable timber-frame buildings from the Middle Ages and high-level walkways remain.

Liverpool holds different memories – of melancholia, urban decay, the sea and flight. One of my first memories is of a ride on a bus on a cold and wet winter afternoon, looking at the grey, drab city through the condensation on the window. I recently saw *Don't Look Back* again, a film from 1965 by D. A. Pennebaker on Bob Dylan's tour of the UK, and it brought back the atmosphere of the city I remember from my childhood.

In time, I have come to appreciate that subtle urban concept many British cities display: the Picturesque. In the case of London, the parts of the city that developed in the eighteenth and nineteenth centuries generally reflected older field patterns and forms of land ownership. Much of the compositional character of London comes from this older landscaping tradition, and the Picturesque is arguably one of Britain's greatest contributions to urban culture. It developed as a way of organising the elements that form a landscape in a manner that evokes a sense of naturalness, a sort of accidental quality. For instance, the planting of trees in a cluster suggests that they are self-seeded and determined by nature, rather than a man-made construct. Similarly, in the planning of British towns and cities, institutional buildings are embedded in the urban fabric rather than placed at the end of a long axis, as they are elsewhere in Europe. The compositional character of urban development operates in parallel to the Picturesque landscaping sensibility, which Robert Maxwell aptly described as 'careful carelessness'.

As a compositional device, the Picturesque is more in line with the ancient Greeks' way of city building, rather than the Romans', who strove to create subtle and harmonious spatial relationships between buildings, and would make conscious adjustments to reinforce the intended effect.

For the last four years, I have been living in Zurich, and have enjoyed being in central Europe, in close proximity to German, French and Italian cultures. My weekly working pattern involves travelling from the north to the south of the Alps to Mendrisio, where I teach, and every few weeks I go back to London. While I find it stimulating to move so freely from one urban centre to another, I cannot avoid noticing that all is not well with the European city.

It is shocking to consider that more has been built in the world in the period that followed the Second World War than in the entire history of human settlement, especially as so much of what has been built is – at least in my opinion – of poor quality, both in terms of energy efficiency and of architectural quality. It would be naive and perhaps inappropriate to expect all contemporary buildings to be architectural masterpieces. As Lampugnani reminds us, in the past the repetition of known building types was imbued with moral and ethical purpose. I would argue that the contemporary fascination with individualism and the obsessive search for originality results in cultural impoverishment, rather than in better urban conditions.

As Roger Diener writes,"town planning attains its essence in those situations when it can bring a place to order with one house".[2] Swiss cities demonstrate how individual responsibility and collective action can deliver remarkable results. It would be easy to dismiss this as merely a consequence of Switzerland's affluence. The economic circumstances of London are equivalent, but outcomes have proved very different.

2 Roger Diener and Martin Steinmann, *The House and the City*, Birkhäuser Verlag, Basel 1995, 10

Rykwert reminds us that we are all responsible in small and large ways for the shaping and character of the cities we live in:

> Although no town or city I live in can possibly be exactly as I wish it, even in the best of all possible worlds, yet the way it looks and the way it works has been determined by people like myself, not by impersonal forces: you and I also made the decisions, however small – how to fence a garden, what car to buy, which way to vote in local elections – that go to make up the physical shape of the city. What sometimes

looks like an impersonal force is often a vector such as I have described, resulting from all our decisions, whose exact angle or direction as well as impact we inevitably modify by our everyday activities, however subtly.[3]

3 Joseph Rykwert, *The Seduction of Place: The History and Future of The City*, Oxford University Press, Oxford 2004, 10

I have spent the greater part of my life in one or another version of the European city. And it is through this ever-evolving relationship and through my work as an architect that I have developed a great fascination for the myriad of urban centers in this relatively small but historically significant continent. Indeed, I am grateful for a working life that constantly exposes me to the many and varied cities of Europe.

Some of these cities are now old friends that I find myself returning to time and time again. These experiences have left a profound mark on me at a personal level and have shaped my approach to architecture. I am constantly looking for the elements that define the cities I encounter, and consider the way these might be interpreted critically and made relevant to our work. For simply copying would not make sense, even if it does have a long tradition in all forms of art practice.

What I do is look, and attempt to understand the intrinsic quality of something that exists in a place, a building or an element of a building, and later attempt to recreate it in a manner that is relevant to the projects I am exploring. In this way, the mimetic nature of drawing upon known things leads to new interpretations. I would argue that this is consistent with the foundation on which art practice has been based for thousands of years: a body of knowledge that is there to be learnt from, rather than dismissed outright.

A version of this text was given as a lecture by the same title in Prague on 2 March 2017

Acknowledgements

I would like to thank Yvonne Farrell and Shelley McNamara for inviting me to take part in the Special Section, The Practice of Teaching at the 16th International Architecture Exhibition – La Biennale di Venezia 2018 they are directing, and I am grateful to Emmett Scanlon for the great support he has offered in coordinating our exhibit.

I am indebted to Thomas Kramer, Patrick Schneebeli and their team at Park Books for so expertly managing the production and printing of this publication; I am delighted we have been able to work again with this great Swiss publishing house.

I would also like to express my gratitude to my colleagues at the Accademia di architettura, in particular Riccardo Blumer, Marco Della Torre, and the Mendrisio Academy Press (MAP) who generously supported this publication, and to my teaching assistants, Maria Seline Aejmelaeus-Lindström, Jeanne Wellinger, Taro Sakurai and Michael Stettler.

A special word of thanks is also due to to Francesco Tencalla for his invaluable help in realising our exhibit in Venice.

As always, I am grateful to my partners Stephen Bates and Mark Tuff, and to a number of collaborators in the Zurich studio who have helped coordinate the exhibition, notably Flavia Saggese, Sibe Dijster, Jack Seibold Dalla Santa and, above all, Marina Aldrovandi for the wonderful job she has done in project managing this publication.

I am also grateful to the Accademia di architettura and Pro Helvetia for offering their financial support, and to Anna Schindler, Pascal Hunkeler and David Ganzoni at the City of Zurich for their encouragement.

Last, but not least, I am obliged to Roger Diener and his colleagues, and to Martin Steinmann for unwittingly being involved in this project.

The book accompanies the exhibition Teaching/Practice, part of the Special Section, The Practice of Teaching, at the 16th International Architecture Exhibition – La Biennale di Venezia 2018.

Concept: Jonathan Sergison
Book design: Cartlidge Levene
Photography: Bertie Miller, Watermill
Editing: Marina Aldrovandi
Lithography, printing and binding: DZA Druckerei zu Altenburg GmbH, Altenburg, Thuringia, Germany

Photographic credits for "Twenty-one lessons learnt"
4b, 12, 17, 20 Hélène Binet
7, 11a, 11b, 14c Ioana Marinescu
10a, 10b Richard Learoyd
15 Kristien Daem
16 Danko Stjepanovic

The author gratefully acknowledges those who have granted permission to reproduce copyrighted images and apologises for any errors or omissions.

ISBN 978-3-03860-113-5

www.sergisonbates.co.uk

Park Books
Niederdorfstrasse 54
8001 Zurich
Switzerland
www.park-books.com

Park Books is being supported by the Federal Office of Culture with a general subsidy for the years 2016–2020.

This publication has been made possible by the Accademia di architettura – Università della Svizzera italiana.

Accademia
di
architettura